A KID'S GUIDE TO

SAVING *the* PLANET

IT'S NOT HOPELESS AND WE'RE NOT HELPLESS

by Paul Douglas

illustrated by Chelen Écija

beaming ☀ books
MINNEAPOLIS

For my grandson Jordan . . .
and everyone who comes next.
– PD

Text copyright © 2022 Paul Douglas
Illustrations by Chelen Écija, copyright © 2022 Beaming Books

28 27 26 25 24 23 22   1 2 3 4 5 6 7 8

Hardcover ISBN: 978-1-5064-6639-2
eBook ISBN: 978-1-5064-6890-7

Library of Congress Cataloging-in-Publication Data

Names: Douglas, Paul, 1958- author. | Écija, Chelen, illustrator.
Title: A kid's guide to saving the planet : it's not hopeless and we're not
   helpless / by Paul Douglas ; illustrated by Chelen Écija.
Description: Minneapolis, MN : Beaming Books, 2022. | Includes
   bibliographical references. | Audience: Ages 9-13 | Summary: "Nationally
   recognized meteorologist Paul Douglas clearly and thoughtfully presents
   the daunting problems of climate change and offers realistic solutions
   and actions that kids can participate in now"-- Provided by publisher.
Identifiers: LCCN 2021016973 (print) | LCCN 2021016974 (ebook) | ISBN
   9781506466392 (hardcover) | ISBN 9781506468907 (ebook)
Subjects: LCSH: Climatic changes--Juvenile literature.
Classification: LCC QH543 .D68 2022 (print) | LCC QH543 (ebook) | DDC
   577.2/2--dc23
LC record available at https://lccn.loc.gov/2021016973
LC ebook record available at https://lccn.loc.gov/2021016974

VN0004589; 9781506466392; FEB2022

Beaming Books
PO Box 1209
Minneapolis, MN 55440-1209
Beamingbooks.com

TABLE OF CONTENTS

INTRODUCTION

I am a meteorologist in the Twin Cities of Minnesota, where I've been tracking weather for a long time. In fact, it was the weather that convinced me that our climate is changing. Normally, the weather follows a natural rhythm, but it has been playing more and more out of tune since the late 1900s. Something is off. Not just in my home state, but everywhere, it seems.

"Global weirding," or symptoms of a rapidly changing climate, is showing up in the increasingly funky weather floating above our homes. Extreme natural events are now even more severe. They are more costly, more disruptive. Climate change often hits home when it hits home, or maybe when it hits the home of someone you care about.

There's plenty of gloom and doom out there, but remember this: the world isn't ending—it's warming.

This will result in more negative consequences, including more floods, longer heat waves, and freshwater shortages. But most people are keeping their eyes wide open and paying closer attention to what scientists say. They are stepping up to be part of the solution—and you can too.

Young readers give me hope that we will figure this out, possibly sooner than most people realize. Your generation is less skeptical about science, less cynical about the future. You will be the ones who go from debating the science to creating a better world, one that is cleaner, greener, and more sustainable—and you are already making a difference. This book shines a light on young people already stepping up in their communities, and their technology and activism give us hope. We can have everything we want and need but burn fewer fossil fuels, with less pollution of air, water, and climate. *We just need to go faster.*

We will figure out solutions to the climate crisis. And YOU will lead the way. Remember this: *the situation isn't hopeless, and we aren't helpless.*

THE WORLD IS WARMING

Think about the story of Goldilocks. Earth's distance from the sun is just right. Venus is too close to our nearest star. Its oceans bubble and sizzle. Mars is too far away from the sun, causing the planet to freeze every night.

Not only is Earth the perfect distance from the sun, but this magnificent Blue Marble has a delicately thin protective shield: a 30-mile-thick atmosphere of gases and water vapor that make all life possible. The greenhouse gases floating overhead, including carbon dioxide (CO_2) and methane, act as one massive greenhouse, trapping the sun's warmth and re-radiating solar energy back down to the ground. This is a good thing, because the temperature of outer space is a freeze-dried, gasp-worthy -454°F!

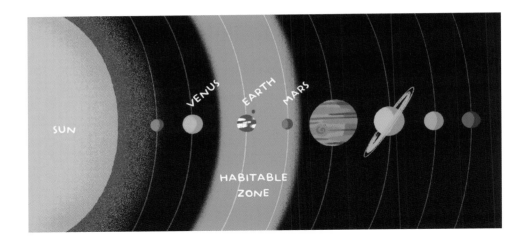

Natural greenhouse gases are the perfect chemical blanket, keeping temperatures relatively stable for thousands of years. Unfortunately, human-made gases have thrown on too many blankets, increasing the greenhouse effect. The burning of coal, oil, and natural gas has released massive amounts of additional CO_2 into our skies. According to NASA, temperatures have warmed roughly 2°F worldwide since 1880, and most of this warming has been observed just since the 1980s.

Scientists track temperature changes in a few ways. Weather buoys at sea measure ocean water temperatures, and unblinking weather satellites orbit Earth, scanning the planet in real time.

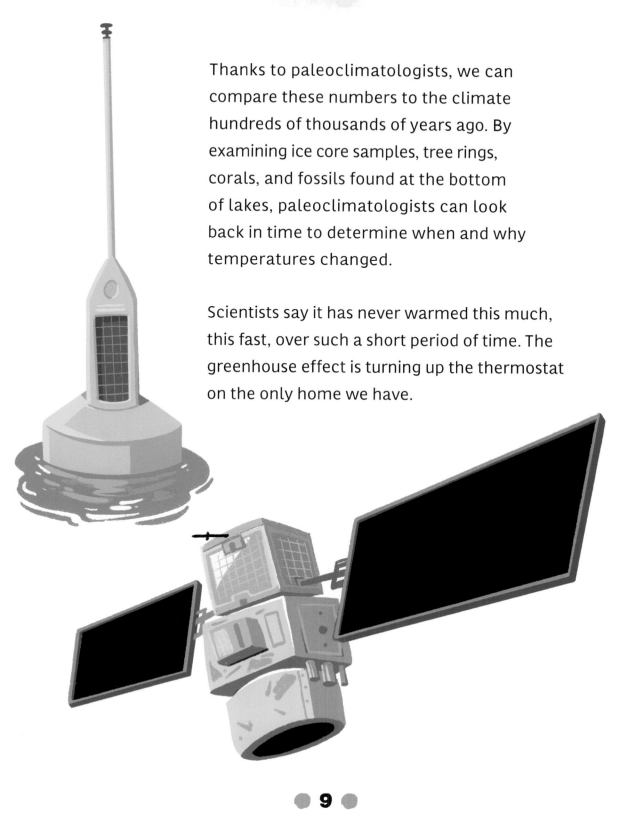

Thanks to paleoclimatologists, we can compare these numbers to the climate hundreds of thousands of years ago. By examining ice core samples, tree rings, corals, and fossils found at the bottom of lakes, paleoclimatologists can look back in time to determine when and why temperatures changed.

Scientists say it has never warmed this much, this fast, over such a short period of time. The greenhouse effect is turning up the thermostat on the only home we have.

HOW DO WE KNOW THE WARMING IS HUMAN-MADE?

The climate has always changed! Volcanoes, the amount of sunlight reaching Earth, and slight wobbles in Earth's orbit around the sun have created big swings in temperature in the past—millions of years ago it was even warmer than it is today. To study the Ice Ages, scientists drill into thick ice over Greenland and Antarctica. Like tree trunks, ice cores have yearly layers. Tiny bubbles of air trapped inside each of these layers make it possible to measure the concentrations of CO_2 year by year. Scientists at NASA now believe the current level of CO_2, which has increased 50% in less than 200 years, is higher than any time in the last 5 million years.

WHERE DO THESE GASES COME FROM? Methane escapes from oil rigs, farming releases CO_2 from the soil, and deforestation, the cutting down of trees and other plants, limits how much CO_2 can be pulled out of the sky and converted to oxygen. Every time we drive a gasoline-powered vehicle, fire up a coal-burning power plant, or activate our natural gas-powered furnaces, we release more CO_2 and other planet-warming greenhouse gases into the atmosphere. How much? Between human-made CO_2 and methane, nearly 50 billion tons of warming gases are released into our atmosphere and oceans every year. (Picture a sky packed with hot-air balloons of CO_2 and methane.)

Why should we care? History shows us that when CO_2 goes up, so does the temperature. When CO_2 falls, temperatures fall. By turning fossilized plants (oil, coal, and natural gas) into the fuels used to power the world, we sparked the climate crisis. A fossil-fueled world was handy, it was cheap, and we ignored the negative impacts (air pollution and warming) until we couldn't anymore.

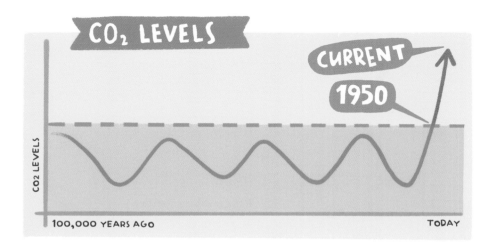

CO₂ LEVELS

CURRENT

1950

CO2 LEVELS

100,000 YEARS AGO

TODAY

Global temperatures are now rising faster than any time in recorded history. The twentieth century was the warmest in 1,000 years. The last decade, since 2010, was the warmest ever observed, and 2020 tied 2016 as the warmest year on record. This might sound great if you live in a cold state, but a rapidly warming planet creates new opportunities, risks, and threats. The good news is that solutions exist. We have all the technology we need to reduce greenhouse warming and cool the planet over time.

WHAT ABOUT VOLCANOES? Hundreds of millions of years ago, when Earth experienced swarms of planetary volcanic eruptions, the climate was even warmer than today. But today fossil fuel emissions are 100 times greater than volcanic releases of CO_2 and methane. During an average year, the state of Florida alone releases more CO_2 than the world's volcanoes. No, it's not volcanoes either. It is us. We are the volcano.

HOW A WARMING WORLD
FLAVORS THE WEATHER

Climate scientists around the world tell us it has never warmed this fast, over such a short period of time. Now let's be real: when a big cold front arrives in the middle of winter, the thought of a warmer world sounds pretty good. But we shouldn't forget the difference between weather and climate. Weather is random and very hard to predict beyond a week or two. Climate responds to the effects of the amount of sunlight reaching the ground, volcanic eruptions, small changes in Earth's orbit around the sun, and the amount of greenhouse gases floating overhead.

Think of weather as a single sneeze and climate as a five-day illness. The overall planet has warmed about 2°F to date, but it's closer to 3–7°F warmer in northern latitudes. When was the last time you were three degrees warmer than usual? You were running a fever, and chances are you felt miserable. And there were obvious symptoms: a runny nose, lack of an appetite, a headache or body aches, maybe sneezing and wheezing. It's the same with Earth: warming is producing observable symptoms. If the climate changes, so will daily weather over time. But they are not the same thing.

A few degrees can make a big difference! It only took a temperature drop of about 12°F to trigger the last Ice Age. Ten thousand years ago, Earth was likely about as warm as it is today, but back then, the slide into a warmer Earth was gradual. The current spike in global temperature is abrupt and unique in our planet's history. If you look carefully, you can already see the effects of rapid climate change showing up today.

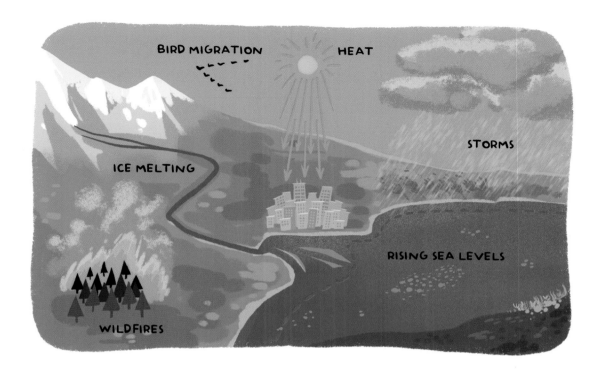

When you're sick, you go to a doctor, who examines your symptoms and comes up with a diagnosis. What is making you sick? A warming Earth has created numerous symptoms that scientists (think of them as doctors keeping an eye on the entire planet) can track over time. A warmer atmosphere and warmer oceans are causing melting glaciers, rising sea levels, hotter heat waves, drier droughts, and stronger storms. Tracking the effects of a warming climate on weather patterns is an opportunity for meteorologists to join climate scientists, to educate people about shifts in weather and how we can prepare for what comes next. The weather is different; it's more extreme more often. Here's how.

⭐ **BILLION-DOLLAR WEATHER DISASTERS INCREASING.**
In the United States, the average was six emergency declarations
every year between 1990 and 1999, but we went up to fifteen
issued each year between 2000 and 2009. Geophysical risks like
volcanoes and earthquakes are holding nearly steady, but flooding,
hurricanes, heat-related deaths, and wildfires are becoming more
frequent over time.

More people live in areas
prone to disaster, next to
rivers threatened by floods
or coastlines in the path
of hurricanes. As a result,
millions of people around
the world lose their homes
every year.

THE NATIONAL WEATHER SERVICE reported a
record twenty-two separate billion-dollar weather and
climate disasters in the US in 2020. That was also the
sixth consecutive year (2015–2020) in which ten or more
billion-dollar weather and climate disaster events had
impacted the United States.

⭐ **RAIN FALLING HARDER.** A warmer atmosphere can hold more water vapor for storms of all shapes and sizes to tap into, from 5-mile-wide thunderstorms to 700-mile-wide hurricanes.

Warmer temperatures mean more water vapor floating overhead to "juice" storms and make it rain harder and longer. Climate scientists predicted 30 to 40 years ago that wet areas would get wetter and dry areas would become drier. That is exactly what has happened. Most of the nation, especially east of the Rocky Mountains, is trending much wetter over time. The Midwest and the Ohio Valley are seeing the biggest increases in extreme rains capable of severe flooding. A warmer, wetter atmosphere is making it rain harder, especially during the warm season, and East Coast snowstorms are dumping more, heavier snow. More snow days? Perhaps, especially over northern states.

WHEN IT RAINS, IT POURS. A greater percentage of the United States is experiencing extreme rainfall amounts capable of serious urban and river flooding. Nature never moves in a perfectly straight line, but if you step back, you can track broad trends over time. Since 2010, the most extreme rains impact twice as much of the US as they did from the 1930s to the 1970s. As a result, historic flash floods have struck Baltimore, Nashville, New York City, New Orleans, Houston, Detroit, Atlanta, Tampa, Boulder, the Carolinas, and much of Texas in recent years. Has your hometown been hit by unusual flooding in recent years? You're not alone.

⭐ **AN UNPREDICTABLE JET STREAM.** Our amazing planet has always experienced floods, droughts, and epic storms. But lately it seems like someone secretly turned up the volume on weather mayhem. Extremes have become more extreme over time. Some of these changes in weather may be due to the rate of warming, which is higher in the Arctic and far northern latitudes than near the equator.

These changes may be impacting the shape and speed of the jet stream—the high-speed river of air that dips and loops around Earth, pushing weather systems along in the process. A loopier jet stream, possibly caused by rapid warming of the Arctic, may be causing weather systems to move slower, prolonging floods and droughts in the process. Ask a meteorologist and they'll tell you the truth: when weather slows or stalls, bad things often happen.

Rapid warming of the Arctic triggered an extreme dip in the jet stream that brought bitter air as far south as the Gulf of Mexico in February 2021, creating snow, ice, and extended power outages in Texas that led to the deaths of hundreds of people. In March 2021, severe flash floods impacted Nashville, Tennessee, one of many communities affected by weather-weirding in recent decades. A wavy, loopy jet stream has interrupted the normal rhythm of the weather. Weather patterns are often "all or nothing," alternating between flood and drought. Our weather, increasingly, is playing out of tune.

⭐ **STRONGER HEAT WAVES, LONGER DROUGHTS, AND MORE INTENSE WILDFIRES.** Due to global warming, rare and extreme heat waves impact a percentage of Earth ten times greater than they did from 1951 to 1980. Since 2010, the lower forty-eight US states saw new record-high temperatures consistently outnumbering new record lows by a ratio of two to one. A greater percentage of the US has been experiencing either extreme drought or extreme flooding since 1910. Everyone, it seems, has an extreme weather story, and those extremes are trending more extreme over time.

ONE WAY OF LOOKING AT THE RATE OF WARMING is to look at the mid-latitudes of the Northern Hemisphere. Imagine walking south (toward the equator) from your home about 30 feet every day of the year. It would get warmer the farther south you walked, right? That's the rate of warming your hometown is experiencing, a slow-motion warming trend that often gets hidden in day-to-day weather changes.

As droughts are becoming more frequent, lasting longer, and impacting more people, wildfires have also doubled in the US. Since the 1980s, the length of the wildfire season has grown by more than two months. The western US has seen a series of devastating wildfires in recent years, made worse by a warmer, drier climate.

⭐ **MORE INTENSE HURRICANES.** The largest, most fearsome storms on Earth, hurricanes, get their energy from warm ocean water. The warmer and deeper the layer of water below, the more intense these storms can become. The 2020 Atlantic tropical season was the most active and the fifth costliest on record, with a total of thirty tropical storms and hurricanes. Scientists predict that we may see fewer hurricanes in the years ahead, but the storms that do spin up will be stronger, be capable of higher winds, and bring ashore a more severe surge of water and much heavier inland rains.

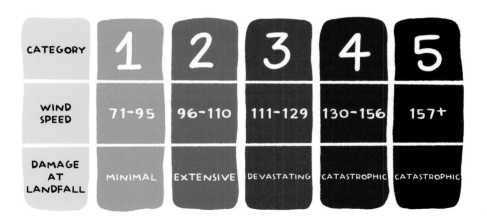

CATEGORY	1	2	3	4	5
WIND SPEED	71-95	96-110	111-129	130-156	157+
DAMAGE AT LANDFALL	MINIMAL	EXTENSIVE	DEVASTATING	CATASTROPHIC	CATASTROPHIC

Today, many hurricanes are supersized, and lighter jet stream winds during late summer and autumn may be causing these massive storms to slow down and even stall for days at a time. A warmer atmosphere and ocean mean more moisture available for hurricanes, and if they move slower during summer and fall, they can drop more rain, increasing the potential for historic flooding.

Due to unusually warm water near the coast, a weak hurricane can escalate into a monster Category 4 storm overnight, trapping hundreds of thousands of people on vulnerable barrier islands, unable to drive inland in time to escape a sudden superstorm. Research suggests we are experiencing more hurricanes that intensify rapidly as they approach the US shoreline, fueled by warmer water.

IN AUGUST 2017, HURRICANE HARVEY soaked coastal Texas with as much as 60 inches of rain. Most hurricanes dump out approximately 10–20 inches. The rain from Hurricane Harvey was about three times the typical amount and 15% more intense because of climate change.

⭐ **SEA-LEVEL RISE.** As water warms, it expands. Since water can't expand downward, global warming causes water levels to rise over time. In addition, most of the world's glaciers are melting, including the largest sources of ice: Antarctica and Greenland. Remember that warm blanket of human-made greenhouse gas chemicals we talked about? Of the

additional warming from burning fossil fuels, most is going into the world's oceans, which are rising rapidly and becoming more acidic over time, threatening all aquatic life. As this warmer water and air reach Greenland, Antarctica, and the world's glaciers, the melting of ice speeds up sea-level rise. It's a vicious cycle.

Worldwide, the average sea-level rise is 8 inches since 1880, but some coastal areas are seeing a much faster uptick in water levels due to local factors such as land subsidence. Subsidence means that due to development (more buildings being constructed) and pumping drinking water from underground sources called "aquifers," the land is actually sinking. The ground is sinking at the same time the ocean is rising. NASA suggests that seas are rising at the fastest rate in the last twenty-eight centuries.

And it's happening faster than originally predicted; an additional 3-foot rise by the year 2100 may be, in their words, "unavoidable."

The rise in sea levels makes the impact of hurricane storm surges and even regular storms worse. Coastal "nuisance flooding" is increasing, not just in the United States but worldwide. From Bangladesh to small island nations in the Pacific Ocean, rising seas are a slow-motion threat. Nearly 150 million people around the world live within 3 feet of sea level. Many of them will have to move in the years ahead, triggering more mass migrations and possible unrest.

Some parts of the US are more vulnerable than others, including coastal Louisiana, the Tidewater region of Virginia, and south Florida. In Miami it routinely floods on a clear day with no storms nearby, just a full moon and tidal tug, all due to rising sea levels!

Climate migration is already happening around the world, and experts believe millions of people will have to move to escape rising seas and increasingly hot summers in decades to come.

SINCE 1959, WHEN ALASKA BECAME A STATE, 3.5 trillion tons of ice have melted from Alaska's glaciers. That's enough water to fill more than a billion Olympic-size swimming pools! It is estimated that as many as 90% of the world's glaciers may be lost in the next few centuries if heat-trapping greenhouse gases continue to rise at current rates.

THE POLLUTED STATES
OF AMERICA

Water and air, the two essential fluids on which all life depends, have become global garbage cans.

—JACQUES COUSTEAU, FRENCH CONSERVATIONIST, AUTHOR, AND FILMMAKER

When I was 10 years old, I went to Pittsburgh, Pennsylvania, on a business trip with my father. I remember that the downtown skyline was hard to see through a thick curtain of smoke and haze. When I got home, my white T-shirt was stained orange. It was from pollution—steel mills belching endless clouds of grit and grime.

We live on a polluted planet. Some say it is a necessary evil, an inescapable side effect of modern life. Creating new products and services, commuting, traveling, farming, and consuming result in waste, and a lot of that waste is harmful to humans and the amazing planet we call home.

A RIGHT TO BREATHE CLEAN AIR

We can never take clean air for granted. According to the World Health Organization, dirty air results in 7 million premature deaths every year. Nine out of ten people living on this planet consistently breathe air containing high levels of pollution. In the United States, air pollution alone kills an estimated 200,000 people each year. Breathing in polluted air is bad for our health. Long-term exposure to air pollution has been associated with diseases of the heart and lungs, cancers, and other health problems. That's why it is important for us to monitor air pollution.

Air pollution is caused by solid, liquid, and certain gas particles that are suspended in the air. These particles can come from car and truck exhaust, factories, and natural sources like dust, pollen, mold spores, volcanoes, and wildfires. The solid and liquid particles suspended in our air are called aerosols. Aerosols are formed from chemical reactions, like the ones that take place when we burn fossil fuels, including oil, gas, and coal—or even just wood. Car exhaust, factories, wildfires, and volcanoes can all pump aerosols into the air. We cannot stop a volcano, but new technologies can reduce or even eliminate human-made air pollution over time.

Certain gases can cause pollution and affect human health, increasing the risk of lung disease. For example, ozone is important to have in the stratosphere, 20–50 miles above the ground, because it screens out harmful ultraviolet radiation from the sun. But near the ground, ozone is created when sunlight reacts with chemicals that come from burning fossil fuels, such as from factories or car exhaust. The result is smog, which can irritate lungs and make it hard for some people to breathe.

Because of bad air, one in thirteen Americans—more people than ever before—suffer from asthma. Asthma can make it difficult for people to catch their breath, and we have no cure for it, only treatments. Asthma is now the number-one reason kids miss school in the United States.

The air overhead is cleaner than it was in 1970, when the Clean Air Act was passed by Congress. But it is still not nearly clean enough. A transition away from fossil fuels toward clean, renewable energy sources will lower air pollution over time, but many cities and communities downwind of heavy industry and coal-fired power plants will struggle with dirty air for years to come. Many of those communities are home to people of color, who are much more likely to be impacted by pollution.

LIA HAREL is 18 years old and one of the founders of Minnesota Can't Wait, a youth-led movement working for climate action. Lia is pushing for new laws to phase out fossil fuels and accelerate clean-energy solutions, organizing rallies at the state Capitol, leading marches, testifying in government committee hearings, publishing opinion articles in newspapers, and helping write the framework for a Minnesota Green New Deal bill.

CLEAN WATER IS A HUMAN RIGHT

Our bodies are mostly water, and so is 70% of Earth's surface. Most of that comes from our planet's oceans. Oceans absorb excess CO_2 in the atmosphere, but the world's oceans can only soak up so much. Today, our oceans absorb about a third of human-created CO_2 emissions—about 9 billion tons every year. The result: surface water in the oceans is 30% more acidic than it was just 200 years ago. Aquatic life, from plankton to fish, crabs, and eels, is already being impacted by more acidic water. The changes brought about by human-made greenhouse gases being flushed into the seas threaten coral reefs, biodiversity, and the food chain we depend on to feed a hungry world.

Only 2.5% of Earth's water is drinkable fresh water, and most of that is trapped in polar ice and glaciers. Only 1% of all water is easily accessible for drinking, washing, and farming, and it's been recycled over many millennia. The water you drink today may be hundreds of millions of years old, from when dinosaurs roamed the planet!

We take clean, safe water coming out of our faucets for granted, but pollution, drought, inefficiency, and waste threaten our water more and more. According to the United Nations, by 2025 nearly 2 billion people will live in areas plagued by water scarcity. Two-thirds of people on the planet will be living in water-stressed areas due to use, population, growth, and climate change.

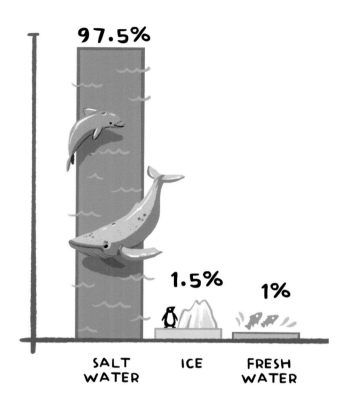

97.5%

1.5%

1%

SALT WATER   ICE   FRESH WATER

Do you look forward to swimming at your favorite lake? Do not take clean, unpolluted water for granted. Approximately 40% of rivers and 46% of lakes in the US are too polluted for fishing, aquatic life, or swimming. Be careful before you dash into that crashing surf: one in ten beaches in the United States fails to meet the federal benchmark for safe swimming water.

Every day, 2 million tons of sewage and other human-made sources of pollution drain into the world's waters. And every single year, 1.2 trillion gallons of untreated sewage, stormwater, and industrial waste are dumped into US water.

The statistics really make your head spin! Roughly 860 billion gallons of tainted water overflow from sewer systems across America, winding up in our waterways. The number-one cause of water pollution in the US: domestic wastewater and sewage, since it makes up 80% of all water pollution. Groundwater is also vulnerable to pesticide and fertilizer runoff that drains into the ground, along with all the pollution the rain brings down. That is a big problem, since roughly half of the United States gets its water from underground aquifers: layers made of sand, clay, and rock, hundreds of feet below the ground, that collect rainwater over many years.

WELL

AQUIFER

Water pollution can come from a specific point source, like a chemical factory or sewage treatment plant—or a non-point source, like rainy runoff from an urban area or chemicals draining from a farming region. Point sources are relatively easy to track down, but non-point sources are difficult to spot and control; they usually reach bodies of water by runoff after heavy rains. Synthetic fertilizers and toxic herbicides, insecticides, and pesticides are sprayed on fields, and rain can wash these toxic chemicals into the nearest creeks and rivers, where they are carried downstream.

Having too many pollutants can result in too many nutrients in a lake or other body of water. This leads to a dense growth of plant life, which then causes animals in the water to die from lack of oxygen. This is often the result of too much nitrogen from commercial fertilizer and animal manure from agribusiness.

Polluted water can also lead to disease and death. Every year, more people die from unsafe water than from all forms of violence, including war. The challenge is most severe in developing countries, but the United States is not immune to waterborne diseases.

LAKE

A watershed is an area of land that drains all the streams and rainfall to a common body of water. Managing the US's watersheds is critical; something as simple as maintaining watersheds can serve as a natural filtration system. Smart development in cities can take advantage of trees, permeable pavements, green roofs, and rain gardens to increase water quality over time. Phasing out fossil fuels for clean, renewable energy sources will reduce oil spills and groundwater pollution from fracking natural gas. Fracking is a process that pumps water and harmful chemicals deep underground to push natural gas to the surface.

And sustainable farming with less dependence on nitrogen-based chemicals will help to clean up our country's waterways and make sure you—and future kids—can play in clean, uncontaminated water. People are increasingly realizing that clean air and clean water are not a privilege. They are basic human rights—ones we are going to have to fight for in the years ahead.

AEON BASHIR founded Aeon for Ocean when he was only 7 years old. Aeon's natural curiosity has taken him on multiple whale-watching tours, as well as to beach cleanups and marine conservation meetings. Since its beginning, the Aeon for Ocean organization has grown significantly. Its mission: educating kids about marine life, while focusing on ocean conservation and creating awareness about the importance of oceans within their schools and communities. Aeon believes, "No matter where we live or eat seafood, we all are in trouble when the ocean is in trouble!"

PLASTIC, PLASTIC EVERYWHERE

We have a very serious planetary plastic problem too. Made from fossil fuels, plastics are durable and seem to last forever. They break down very slowly over time. An estimated 90% of all the plastic produced since 1950 is still in existence. We live in an instant-gratification, throwaway world that values convenience over everything else. Half of all plastics ever produced have been manufactured in the last 15 years, and nearly 40% of all plastic made today is single-use plastic bags, wrappers, bottles, and packaging, which linger in landfills for centuries—or often wash into rivers and oceans.

According to *National Geographic*, every year about 8 million tons of plastic escape into oceans from coastal nations. That is the rough equivalent of setting five garbage bags full of trash on every foot of the world's 372,000 miles of coastline around the world!

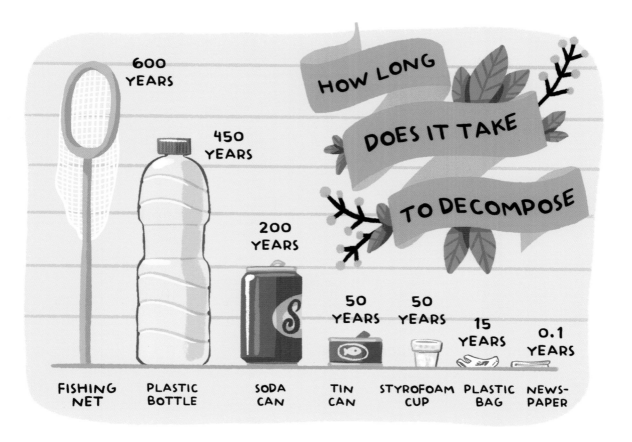

Roughly 80% of all the plastic in our oceans originates on land. The other 20% leaks from ocean-based sources like fisheries and fishing vessels. By 2050, the oceans will likely contain more plastic than fish! There may already be as much as 100 million tons of plastic in the world's oceans, most of it submerged. A floating island of trash in the central Pacific Ocean, called the Great Pacific Garbage Patch, stretches 600,000 square miles, which is more than twice the size of Texas!

Once plastics are washed into the sea, sunlight, waves, and wind break them down into microplastics, some pieces so small they are picked up by the winds and carried all over the planet. Very tiny bits of plastic have even been observed on Earth's tallest mountain, Mount Everest, and found in the deepest part of the ocean, the Mariana Trench. Plastic microfibers have been found in public drinking-water systems and drifting through the air. With plastic particles in our land, air, and water, we are conducting a global experiment on human health. We were not meant to breathe, eat, or drink tiny particles of plastic.

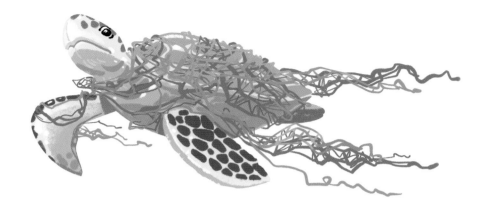

Besides the unknown impact on human health, plastic waste is pervasive and deadly every year for millions of animals, who often die after getting tangled up and strangled in plastic wrappers or by ingesting the plastic. Nearly seven hundred species, including endangered ones, have been affected by plastics. More than one hundred aquatic species have been found with microplastics in their digestive tracts, including shrimp, mussels, and fish, which ultimately wind up in grocery stores and restaurants, and on our dining room tables.

Recycling is only part of the solution and, sadly, the world is running out of space to store all the plastic waiting to be recycled. Only 8.4% of the plastic waste in the US was recycled in 2017. New, plastic-free package design, and movement away from wasteful single-use containers, will be essential to keep plastic out of our land, air, and water in the years to come.

FIONN FERREIRA was kayaking near his home in West Cork, Ireland, when he spotted a rock covered in tiny bits of plastic. Inspired, he created a mixture of oil and magnetite that, when added to the water, created a magnetic effect that removed 87% of the microplastics. Fionn hopes to work with wastewater plants to remove plastic particles before they are released into rivers and oceans. "I'm not saying that my project is the solution," he told *Business Insider*. "The solution is that we stop using plastic altogether."

WE'VE CLEANED UP
OUR MESSES BEFORE

We do not inherit the Earth from our ancestors; we borrow it from our children.

—CHIEF SEATTLE

Climate change, pollution, and plastic everywhere seem like massive, impossible problems to solve. But here's the thing: we've been down this road before. Faced with big, global environmental challenges with no easy answers, we always found a way forward. Working together, we found the solutions we needed to clean up our own messes.

POLLUTION CAN TRIGGER ACID RAIN

When I was a child, one of the big concerns my generation faced was acid rain. Pollution from factories, utilities, and vehicles was mixing with water droplets in the air to create rain with low pH values that killed fish, harmed wildlife, and damaged trees. Normal rain is slightly acidic, with a pH of 5.6, while acid rain generally has a pH between 4.2 and 4.4. (The lower the number on the pH scale, the more acidic something is.)

The primary culprit was the burning of fossil fuels, especially by coal-fired power plants. Among the pollutants released into the air were sulfur dioxide and nitrogen oxide, which—when combined with water droplets—created sulfuric acid and nitric acid.

A steady wind blowing overhead pushed these chemicals hundreds of miles downwind from the pollution source, allowing them to combine with water, oxygen, and other chemicals, eventually falling to the ground as acidic rain, tainting water supplies and stunting trees and other plant life.

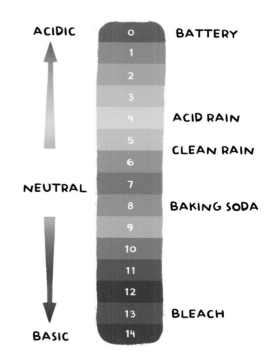

Acid rain and fog can damage forests, especially at higher elevations, and some parts of the US are more vulnerable to the impacts than others. New England is especially prone to the negative effects of acid rain, which can leave trees and plants less healthy and more vulnerable to disease, insects, and cold winter temperatures. The region of the United States most harmed by acid rain is the East Coast, including the Appalachian Mountains and the Northeast.

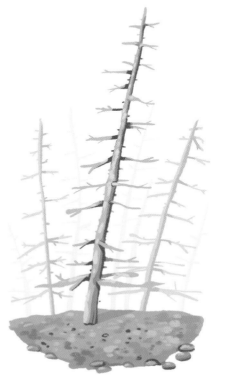

Repeated exposure to acid rain can even corrode concrete. Historical monuments have seen their exteriors partially dissolve over time. The Taj Mahal in India and the Thomas Jefferson Memorial in Washington, DC, are two of many monuments, buildings, and national treasures affected by acid rain. Acids in polluted air react with the calcite in those materials, slowly dissolving them over time, causing surfaces to erode so they lose their sharp details, gloss, color, and delicate carvings. If acid rain can do this to statues over time, imagine what it can do to your favorite lake or forest!

We knew we had a problem with the rain, and scientists were able to connect the dots and explain how the burning of fossil fuels was making our rain more acidic. So, in 1990, Congress passed a law called the Clean Air Act Amendments. This law said that the Environmental Protection Agency, the US government agency that tries to protect our land, air, and water from harmful pollution, should start the Acid Rain Program.

This program limits the amount of sulfur dioxide and nitrogen oxide electricity-producing power plants can release into the air.

Removing impurities from coal, as well as burning coal with less sulfur, helped. Another solution was to install equipment called scrubbers, which removed the sulfur dioxide from gases leaving smokestacks. Today, burning coal to generate electricity is on the decline, so the threat of acid rain is slowly falling over time.

Other solutions came into play too, like cleaner cars with better gas mileage and less pollution leaving the tailpipe. Utilities that generate electricity across the United States are benefiting from a transition to cleaner, cheaper renewable energy, which is driving down air pollution and acid rain. The problem has not entirely gone away, but we are in better shape than we were 50 years ago.

GRETA THUNBERG first heard about climate change when she was 8 years old and could not understand why so little was being done about it. In 2018, at the age of fifteen, Thunberg launched a one-person School Strike for Climate outside the Swedish Parliament, calling on world leaders to do more to battle climate change and heal the planet. Her passion has inspired a global movement of young people demanding accountability and faster action on climate solutions.

We recognized we had a problem with the rain, and the people made their voices heard. Representative democracy worked! Our representatives in Congress passed new laws to lower pollution and clean up the rain, which was better for our health and better for the economy. Good things happen when enough people rise up and demand solutions.

WHO CARES ABOUT AN OZONE HOLE?

Not too long ago, the world had an ozone hole scare. For many decades, chemical reactions involving chlorine and bromine reduced ozone in the upper reaches of our atmosphere, the stratosphere. This lack of stratospheric ozone is called the ozone hole. Because less ozone meant less protection from the sun's harmful ultraviolet rays, the risk of skin cancer and eye cataracts increased.

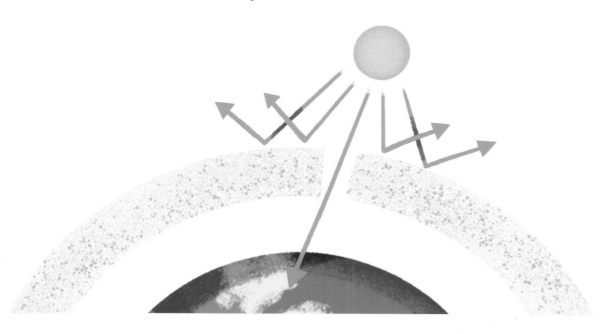

Scientists became increasingly alarmed in the 1980s, warning that depletion of ozone in the stratosphere could harm plants, animals, and even humans on the ground below. Specific chemicals were the culprit: chlorofluorocarbons, or CFCs. At the time, these chemicals were used in hairspray, aerosol cans, and refrigerators. A single CFC molecule can last between 20 and 100 years in the atmosphere and can destroy 100,000 ozone molecules. In 1987, governments around the world banded together to sign the Montreal Protocol, a global treaty that phased out the use of these harmful chemicals over time.

As countries across the planet recognized an environmental problem, they came together and, after much debate and negotiation, took collective action to solve a huge challenge.

The ozone hole has not totally gone away, but it is smaller than it was in the 1970s and 1980s. This is a remarkable achievement for society, proof that if enough people take notice—and take a stand—steps can be taken to help our planet recover and heal.

We are the problem, and we are the solution.

A CLEAN-ENERGY REVOLUTION:
WE WILL SOLVE THIS PROBLEM

> Our universe is a sea
> of energy—free, clean energy.
> It is all out there waiting for
> us to set sail upon it.
>
> —ROBERT ADAMS

The world is already coming together and getting serious about climate action. A (rising) tide is starting to turn, led by an army of young people not content with denial and delay. They want action and they want it now. We cannot ignore the data or the scientists any longer.

Our planet has already warmed an average of nearly 2°F since the 1800s. Climate scientists warn that we need to keep overall warming to under 2.7°F. That will be difficult, but not impossible. We do not need any new miracle technologies to slow the rate of warming. We have everything we need today—we just need to move faster as the world transitions away from fossil fuels.

Consider this: enough sunlight hits Earth every hour to power the entire world for an entire year! The wind blows consistently, strongly enough to power wind turbines across much of the United States. Although it costs money to install wind turbines and solar panels, the source of energy is nearly limitless, and free to harness, once you have the right equipment in place.

We need smarter, cheaper ways to harvest the sun, the wind, the water (hydropower), the waves (tidal power), and biofuels (plants and algae)—along with new clean-energy sources we can't even imagine, which are coming sooner than you think.

TAKING FULL ADVANTAGE OF SUNSHINE AND WIND. Farmers have been tapping clean, renewable energy for hundreds of years, using windmills for pumping water, while greenhouses take full advantage of free solar power to grow vegetables and flowers year-round.

⭐ **GOING SOLAR.** Solar energy is the most abundant energy resource on Earth—173,000 terawatts of solar energy strike Earth continuously. (A terawatt is 1 trillion watts. A typical light bulb is only 60 watts.) That's more than 10,000 times the world's total energy use. Solar panels, solar shingles, solar paint—why wouldn't we try to harvest free energy hitting our homes?

The amount of solar power installed in the US has increased by more than twenty-three times over the past 8 years, and as innovation accelerates and prices continue to fall, more of us will sign up for sun power!

★ **WIND TURBINES.** Human civilizations have harnessed wind power for thousands of years. A wind turbine has as many as 8,000 different components, and they are big (and getting bigger over time to generate electricity even more efficiently). Wind turbine blades average over 190 feet long, and turbine towers average 295 feet tall—about the height of the Statue of Liberty. Wind power is now the largest source of renewable energy in the US. There was enough wind energy in 2019 to power 29.5 million average American homes. Wind energy provides more than 10% of total electricity in fourteen states and more than 30% in Kansas, Iowa, and Oklahoma. The Great Plains of the United States consistently produce more wind power than nearly any other spot on the planet.

But the wind blows consistently across much of New England, the Appalachians, the Rockies, and the western US as well. We are just now beginning to tap the potential of free wind power.

⭐ **BIOFUELS.** These fuels are like petroleum diesel, but they are created from biomass—renewable resources made by plants and animals (like corn and algae). It is not a perfect source of energy, since farming and processing biofuels emits pollutants like carbon and methane back into the air. But methane gas released through rotting materials in landfills can be used to generate power, and biodiesel fuels made from corn can power cars and trucks to burn more cleanly, with less carbon released into the atmosphere in the short term. They also lower our country's dependence on oil from other nations.

⭐ **HYDROPOWER.** One of the oldest power sources on the planet is hydropower: generating power when flowing water spins a wheel or turbine. It was used by farmers as far back as ancient Greece for mechanical tasks like grinding grain. Hydropower is cheaper than most other energy alternatives. Hydropower provides about 7% of the electricity generated in the United States and about half of the electricity from all renewable sources, according to the Energy Information Administration. Every state uses hydropower for electricity, and some states use a lot of it. Over 70% of Washington State's electricity comes from hydropower, and eleven states get more than 10% of their electricity from hydropower. Another benefit: many dams built for flood control could be used to generate electricity.

★ **ENERGY STORAGE.** It's not your grandfather's batteries anymore. The first battery (called "Volta's cell") was invented in 1800, and innovation has increased how much energy can be stored in a battery. The cost of energy storage (like big batteries that can power cars, homes, and even entire cities) has fallen 76% since 2012.

★ **GEOTHERMAL ENERGY.** The Roman Empire tapped geothermal (meaning "earth heat") power to warm baths! It's another energy source that never runs out because of natural heat found deep underground. Geothermal heat pumps, also known as ground-source heat pumps, can heat, cool, and even supply hot water to a home by sending water deep underground to capture the heat before pumping it back up. This technology has been keeping consumers comfortable for more than 50 years and can cut energy bills by up to 65% compared to traditional heating and cooling units. These pumps can last anywhere from 25 to 30 years, providing heating and cooling for homes year-round.

⭐ **NUCLEAR ENERGY.** A new generation of smaller, cheaper, and safer nuclear plants may be able to provide baseline power, the minimum amount of electric power needed to be supplied to the electrical grid, the network of power stations connected to high-voltage lines that bring electricity into our homes around the clock. Molten-salt reactors, using very hot (liquid) salt as fuel, are much safer than earlier designs that rely on uranium and other toxic elements, because they can cool themselves even if the system loses power completely. This means we wouldn't have the issue of waste, like plutonium (which can be turned into nuclear weapons), falling into the wrong hands. A home run for clean energy is fusion reactors, which mimic the sun. Creating a focused temperature of 150 million degrees Celsius is no small task, but at some point, someone somewhere is going to figure this out! The advantage? No release of greenhouse-warming gases into the atmosphere.

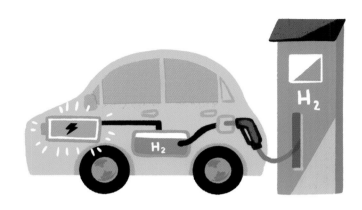

⭐ HYDROGEN AND FUEL CELLS.
Hydrogen is the most abundant element on Earth. Hydrogen can be found in fossil fuels, biomass, and water. Scientists access this hydrogen through a process called electrolysis, which uses electricity to split water into hydrogen and oxygen. Machines called fuel cells then turn that hydrogen into electricity to power everything from vehicles to buildings. Unlike batteries, fuel cells do not run down or need to recharge—as long as there's a constant source of fuel and oxygen.

How are you making the planet a better place? A clean-energy transformation in the business world is happening at breakneck speed. Companies will have to walk the talk if they want to survive and thrive while keeping their customers happy. Reducing their carbon footprint (the amount of CO_2 that goes into the production and transportation of their products) is increasingly mission critical.

⭐ **TIDAL ENERGY.** Thanks to the gravitational tug of the moon, energy from wave power, ocean tides, and currents is limitless. In fact, the total energy contained in tides worldwide is 3,000 gigawatts. A gigawatt is a billion watts, a staggering amount of potential energy.

⭐ **ENCOURAGING TRENDS.** Thanks to these new and improving technologies, clean-energy prices are falling. The cost of solar energy has fallen nearly 80% in a decade. Wind-power costs are lower by 65%, and energy storage is 76% cheaper since 2012. A cleaner, green world is within our grasp, and lower prices make it more possible for more people.

The world needs energy abundance: more energy for less money, with fewer unpleasant side effects. The world is heading toward a no-excuses renewable-energy economy. We aren't able to entirely stop burning oil, gas, and coal—not yet—but these older, dirtier, and more expensive fuels will slowly fade away as newer, cleaner, and cheaper options take their place. The (electric) train is leaving the station and we're all aboard!

AT THE AGE OF SIXTEEN, ANN MAKOSINSKI won a Google Science Fair with a flashlight that runs on heat from a human hand. Ann was inspired by a friend in the Philippines, who was failing school because her family could not afford electricity to light a room for her to study in. In a flash of inspiration, Ann created the flashlight—and a mug that can charge a smartphone using energy from a hot drink. Ann is part of a growing army of young entrepreneurs determined to bring a new, clean-energy economy into the world faster than anyone thought possible.

CLIMATE SOLUTIONS
YOU CAN DO

> Anything's possible if you've got enough nerve.
>
> —J.K. ROWLING

The average American family produces 7.5 tons of CO_2 every year. Each one of us can think of ways to reduce that number, and then put those methods into action. We can take steps today to heal the planet. Some are easier than others, and some will have to wait until you are older, when you can purchase an energy-efficient electric vehicle, put solar panels on your home, or choose a green career. But on the next pages are a whole lot of great ideas for things you can do today. You'll also meet some inspiring young people who are doing great green things to heal our planet.

Remember, the situation isn't hopeless, and we aren't helpless. That's not just a slogan—it's the truth. A clean, green revolution in how we power our homes and drive our vehicles and grow our food is well underway.

⭐ **PLANT A TREE.** Sometimes the simplest ideas are the most powerful. Trees are the perfect carbon-removal devices. They absorb CO_2 and release oxygen. A greater number of trees can remove more carbon from the atmosphere faster. Look into public resources like local clubs that provide trees for planting in your area. If you have a yard, plant trees close to home to provide shade and natural cooling during the summer.

AMIRA QUIÑONES lives in Puerto Rico. After Hurricane Maria in 2017, many of her neighbors struggled with hunger. Amira handed out fruit trees and plants to low-income families as part of an effort called Regreen Puerto Rico. Her goal was to bring native plants back to the island while creating less dependence on imported food. Now a sustainable living coach, Amira focuses on resilience and sustainable solutions that lower the impact of climate change for her home.

SOPHIE BERNSTEIN is focused on "food deserts," areas where stores with affordable, nutritious fruits and vegetables from local sources are hard to find. Sophie launched Grow Healthy, a nonprofit that has created twenty-two vegetable gardens in low-income childcare centers. More than 17,000 pounds of produce have been grown for local food banks. Sophie leads a team of nearly eight hundred volunteers, organizing garden workshops about plant science and sustainable gardening.

⭐ **CONSIDER PLANTING A VEGETABLE GARDEN.** Fresh fruits and vegetables from your local grocery store travel an average of 1,500 miles from the farm to your plate. The more food you grow yourself or purchase from local sources, the less food must be transported on planes, trains, and trucks. This saves energy and is more fun and healthy.

★ **ADJUST YOUR THERMOSTAT** to use less air conditioning during the warm months and less heat during the cool months. Even a few degrees can save money and pump fewer climate-warming greenhouse gases into the sky. Instead of cranking up the air conditioning when it's hot outside, see how long you can go with a fan, which uses a tiny fraction of energy compared to AC. When it turns cold, go old-school by putting on a sweatshirt and socks. Hey, it worked for our ancestors!

★ Talk with your parents or caregivers about upgrading your home with **ENERGY-EFFICIENT LIGHT BULBS.** Swap old incandescent bulbs for new compact fluorescent lights (CFLs). They use 25% as much electricity to give out the same amount of light, and they last ten times longer! Pro tip: they will also save money on electric bills!

⭐ **UNPLUG ELECTRONICS** when not in use, including video games, coffee makers, and smart speakers. Even when turned off, these vampire gadgets "sip" small amounts of electricity. Plug them into a power strip with an on/off switch, so you can turn off all the power without

unplugging every gadget. Turn off lights, TVs, and all other screens and computers when you don't need them.

⭐ Encourage your parents to **CONSIDER AN ELECTRIC VEHICLE** next time they're car shopping. Not everyone can afford one, but prices have come down in recent years. Many electric vehicles (EVs) have a range of over 300 miles, which means they can travel that far without their batteries being recharged. EVs save money on gasoline, insurance, and maintenance. They have far fewer moving parts—which means less that can break!

⭐ **UPGRADE APPLIANCES.** Refrigerators, microwaves, dishwashers, clothes washers, dryers, and in-home air-conditioning units manufactured before 2001 are much less energy efficient than more current appliances. New refrigerators beep if the door is left open. Smartphone apps can alert you if the air conditioner is running when you aren't home.

⭐ **RETHINK YOUR LAUNDRY.** Roughly 75% of total energy use and greenhouse-gas emissions produced by a single load of laundry comes from warming the water. Consider washing in cold water, which is just as effective. Dryers are one of the most energy-hungry appliances. Air-drying your clothes can reduce the average home's carbon footprint by 2,400 pounds a year.

★ **KEEP LIGHTS TURNED OFF WHEN POSSIBLE.** When you're reading or doing homework, find a spot that can take full advantage of (free!) natural light. Windows are marvelous inventions. Use them.

★ **WALK OR RIDE A BIKE.** Cars are big producers of CO_2. Even a short, 2-mile car trip puts 2 pounds of additional CO_2 into the atmosphere. When possible, try walking or biking to replace car trips. Pro tip: it's a much healthier way to get from point A to point B!

★ **USE SMART TRANSPORTATION.** For longer travel, consider taking a train or bus instead of driving or flying to your destination. You'll emit far less CO_2 getting from point A to point B. Something as simple as keeping your car's tires properly inflated can save significant energy over time too.

★ **JUST SAY NO TO THE DRIVE-THRU.** When you go to a fast-food restaurant, park the vehicle and walk inside. Sitting in your car to wait for food means more idling and more pollution.

★ **RECYCLE!** Take time to separate out aluminum cans, cardboard, plastic, glass, newspapers, and junk mail—anything made of paper. This cuts down on waste sent to incinerators and landfills; conserves timber, water, and minerals; saves energy; and prevents pollution.

Starting at the age of three, **RYAN HICKMAN** always accompanied his father to a local recycling center in his hometown of Orange County, California. A few years later he launched Ryan's Recycling. His goal: to intercept cans and bottles before they had a chance to wash into the oceans and damage the environment. He inspired friends, families, and neighbors to chip in and help. Over the years, Ryan and a team of volunteers have collected hundreds of thousands of cans and bottles, raising money for the nearby Pacific Marine Mammal Center.

⭐ **DRINK TAP WATER** in a reusable container. Plastic bottles are a disaster for the planet. Stay hydrated in a smarter way. Here is a dirty little secret: tap water usually tastes just as good as that fancy water you have to pay for.

⭐ **BUY RESPONSIBLY.** Companies are getting better with using less packaging material to ship products, but this is still a global problem. Think of all the trees that went into all that cardboard required to get that new video game to your house. Shop in-store to cut back on those shipping materials, and choose products with less packaging. Keep a dedicated reusable cloth bag on your bike or in the family car to bring items home from the store, to cut down on the need for paper or plastic bags.

★ **SUPPORT COMPANIES THAT ACKNOWLEDGE CLIMATE CHANGE.** Before you buy a product or service, find out if that business is serious about reducing pollution and waste and pushing forward on climate solutions. A simple Google search will answer your questions. More and more companies are stepping up—we should reward the ones that do it right.

★ **BUY LESS.** You are not what you buy. More stuff won't make you genuinely happy—only faith, family, and friends can do that. Instead of purchasing a new item, ask yourself if you can get by with something gently used. Recycle, reuse, and reimagine what you really need and where you can find it. From vintage clothing to recycled furniture, newer is not necessarily better!

★ **INSULATE YOUR HOME.** Making your home more weatherproof can save you big money on heating and cooling expenses throughout the year. That can sometimes mean new windows, but even something as simple as caulking and weather-stripping your home can make a big difference.

MAYA PENN founded Maya's Ideas when she was just 8 years old. She loved fashion, art, and design, but worried about its negative impact on the environment. So, she started a sustainable, handmade clothing line using organic, recycled, and vintage materials. Today, Maya is a celebrity featured on television, on the cutting edge of eco-fashion. She is encouraging her generation to take their passion, experiment, and find new ways to deliver products and services.

★ **TWEAK YOUR WATER HEATER.** Lowering your water temperature from 140°F to 120°F prevents accidental scalding and saves significant energy over time.

⭐ **GO SOLAR!** Clean, green energy is not a fad or a fluke—it is a trend. Why wouldn't we try to harvest the free energy hitting our yards and rooftops? Prices are falling rapidly, and many families are already taking advantage of solar power, wind energy, and energy storage. Ask your parents to encourage the utility that provides your electricity to take full advantage of renewable energy sources.

When **ABBIE WEEKS** discovered an orphanage in Uganda lacking reliable energy, she raised $10,000 and worked with a local trade school in Africa to install a solar energy project. Abbie, a friend, and three teachers flew from her home in Denver, Colorado, to Kampala, bringing 800 pounds of supplies along with them, then drove ten hours by car to deliver aid to the orphanage. Her team didn't leave until the Nyaka AIDS Orphans Project had a reliable, inexpensive, environmentally friendly source of energy.

JADEN ANTHONY has a special passion for comic books and superheroes, and now Jaden is speaking out about climate pollution through his own comic book series, *Kid Brooklyn*. Jaden and his team of close friends use their superpowers to stop an alien race from destroying Earth's natural resources. Highlighting real kids from Brooklyn, New York, the comic series shows the world the power that young people have when they unite for a common purpose. Jaden says you are never too young to have a voice—or to fight for what you believe in.

⭐ **INSPIRE OTHERS!** Share your concerns and ideas about how to make things better. Write a blog post, design posters to hang at school, or record a TikTok to get the word out and challenge others to do their part.

★ **SHARE YOUR CONCERNS.** Author C. S. Lewis said it best: "Nothing is really ours until we share it." Share your concerns, fears, and hopes. Talk it out. Speak up. Raise your voice. If you are worried about climate change, do something and say something. Get your friends and family up to speed. You can do this.

★ **JOIN OR CREATE A CLIMATE CLUB IN YOUR SCHOOL.** Organize. Inform. Act. Make your voice heard, and focus on solutions. Things will not get better if everyone waits for someone else to step up. If you don't have a climate club, start one up yourself. One person can launch a great idea and motivate others!

⭐ **CONSIDER A GREEN CAREER.** If you are passionate about combating climate change or other forms of pollution, consider a job that helps to bring about the future you want—faster. Eleanor Roosevelt, wife of Franklin D. Roosevelt, America's thirty-second president, said, "The future belongs to those who believe in the beauty of their dreams." Bottom line: dream big dreams, but take steps to turn those dreams into reality.

Take the first step and make your own path. Your actions will trigger a chain reaction. Others are watching to see what you will do. Once you get started, you will inspire others to take similar actions. Being part of the solution will not only make you feel good—it will make our inevitable clean-energy future one big step closer!

CLIMATE CAREERS

Choose a job you love, and you will never have to work a day in your life.

—CONFUCIUS

When I was 14 years old, after Tropical Storm Agnes flooded our home in Lancaster, Pennsylvania, I decided I wanted to become a meteorologist—a career in which I learned more about how a warming world affected the weather patterns I was tracking on my maps. As we look to the future, ask yourself how you might use your own passions to make a real difference. This chapter explores some ideas to consider.

Every problem has a solution. Some problems take more time (and money) to cure, but we can do this. I really do believe it, and so should you. You are part of the solution.

- ★ **ARCHITECT.** Drawing up plans to take full advantage of natural sunlight, to disperse water during floods with rain gardens, and to use new materials that are more weatherproof is increasingly important in making our buildings  more flood resistant, heat tolerant, and energy efficient. How can we simultaneously live better and save money on heating and cooling, with less stress, waste, and pollution? Architects are on it.

- ★ **CLIMATE SCIENTIST.** Right now, thousands of climate scientists are conducting research around the world— doing everything from drilling ice core samples to monitoring shifts in rainfall and temperature across the planet in recent decades.

Climate scientists follow the changes that have already taken place, while relying on the latest research and sophisticated climate models to pinpoint future changes and implications.

⭐ **CONSERVATIONIST OR FORESTER.** Shifting rainfall and temperature patterns around the world affect where plants, trees, and animal life can thrive. Conservationists and foresters track these changes over time, suggesting new and innovative ways to protect the natural world around us.

⭐ **ECOTOURISM.** Whether it is visiting nearby states, exploring national parks, or just getting lost in some city on the other side of the planet, there is so much to see! But we can travel more responsibly. Park rangers and tour guides with an appreciation for the environment and sustainability ensure that we can continue to enjoy amazing tourist destinations. People in ecotourism careers help us preserve and protect the places we love so we do not love them to death.

⭐ **ENGINEER.** How do we reduce waste? How can we design entire cities to release fewer greenhouse gases into the atmosphere? From designing more energy-efficient appliances to working on new battery technology that packs even more power and bang for the buck, we need smart people and smart solutions. It is a herculean task, and the US will require a small army of very smart engineers willing to tackle some of the planet's biggest problems.

⭐ **ENVIRONMENTAL ADVOCATE.** Just by reading this book you have already demonstrated an interest in renewability and sustainability. Today, the United States has thousands of nonprofit agencies, like the Sierra Club, the National Audubon Society, and the Evangelical Environmental Network, focused on advocating for positive change: environmental policies that protect Earth while creating more jobs and a sustainable, cleaner-tech economy.

TALK

⭐ **ENVIRONMENTAL LAWYER.** We will always need smart lawyers to enforce existing environmental protections— as well as to draft new laws to protect the air, land, and water. Lawyers advise elected officials while acting as a check on overdevelopment that threatens more pollution and disruption.

⭐ **ENVIRONMENTAL SCIENTIST.** Acid rain. Soil and water contamination. Ozone depletion. The world needs environmental scientists able to design, plan, and apply new methods and materials that reduce pollution and other public-health hazards. That's why your chemistry, biology, and math classes are so important: they give you facts and tools that you can apply in the real world— to make things better!

⭐**FOOD SCIENTIST.** With weather and climate extremes on the increase, how can we engineer crops better able to withstand bigger swings in rainfall and temperature? Indoor farming, immune from crazy weather, is a growing trend. The ability to engineer crops that require less water, or that can better withstand flooding rains, will be an important skill. Food scientists work to ensure we can grow the crops and vegetables we need to feed a hungry world.

⭐ **GOVERNMENT.** A clean-energy future will rely on businesses and governments working together to set new goals and standards while relying on smart companies to produce the products and services we need. You can work for your state's Department of Natural Resources or for federal-government agencies like the Department of Energy (DOE) or the Environmental Protection Agency (EPA).

⭐ **HYDROLOGIST.** People are experiencing frequent flooding in areas that have not flooded in the past, well away from streams and rivers. Predicting which rivers will flood, when, and how bad the flooding will be requires trained professionals who understand the movement of water and its impact hundreds of miles downstream from where a flood is being reported.

⭐ **MAPPING AND GIS CONSERVATION.** Do you like maps? Geographic Information System (GIS) professionals provide the mapping platforms that help us track the changes we are witnessing around the globe. How are floods shifting over time? With the slow-motion warming we are experiencing, what plants and crops can grow in a given area? How might a changing climate impact a certain neighborhood 20 years from now? Maps help tell the story of climate and weather changes.

⭐ **METEOROLOGIST.** The best weather forecasts are a mix of human and machine, experts interpreting current data and weather models, not only to create an accurate prediction but also to warn people when their weather may be life-threatening. New innovations in technology like Doppler radar allow us to zoom down to street level to time when a tornado will hit, or to track which communities are most likely to experience extreme floods. Getting the forecast right is critical, but so is good storytelling—explaining what is happening and why.

⭐ **PHOTOGRAPHER OR FILMMAKER.** Former US vice president Al Gore launched a documentary in 2006 called *An Inconvenient Truth*, highlighting the threat caused by global warming. At the time it was controversial, but many of the warnings and predictions in this film came true, inspiring people to transition from talking about climate change to doing something about human-made global warming. The need for great storytelling will never go away.

⭐ **SCIENCE TEACHER.** If you love science, consider turning that passion into a teaching degree. Someday you will be able to inspire young people to find the tools and solutions we need to clean up the planet and reduce risks posed by pollution and human-made global warming. More discoveries wait to be made. Teachers are an incredibly important part of the solution.

★ **SOLAR PHOTOVOLTAIC INSTALLER.** Consider a career in which you can install solar panels or solar shingles for your neighbors, or design next-generation sun-powered technology that is more powerful (and cheaper!).

★ **WATER AND AIR QUALITY ENGINEER.** We cannot improve or change what we cannot measure. Engineers are essential to tracking levels of pollutants in our air and water. Skills and duties include environmental monitoring, chemical analysis, computer modeling, and statistical analysis.

★ **WIND TURBINE TECHNICIAN.** The professionals who install, inspect, maintain, and operate these enormous wind turbines are well paid, often making six-figure salaries. Like every big machine, turbines require tender loving care to operate at peak efficiency. Parts need replacing, but you don't need a four-year college degree; you can attend a two-year training program at a local technical school or community college to get the skills you need to be successful.

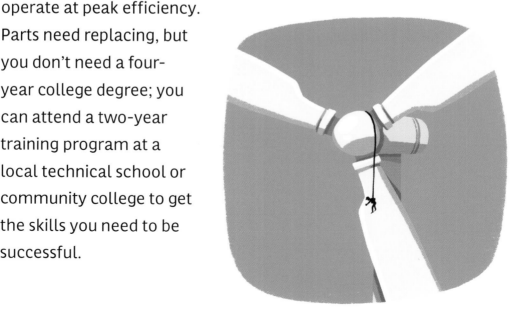

⭐ **WILDLIFE OR MARINE BIOLOGIST.** Wildlife biologists and zoologists study animals to learn how they interact with their ecosystems. Tracking data often requires being out in the field to take measurements and observe animal migrations. Marine biologists do similar work in the oceans. Overfishing, plastic pollution, and higher pH values from warmer, more acidic water are stressing out marine life. If you are good at science and biology in school and you want to find ways to protect animals on land and in the sea, this would be an amazing career option.

⭐ **WRITER AND ECO-JOURNALIST.** Journalists with strong writing skills document the changes we are experiencing, helping us understand why we should pay attention. The internet has a wealth of information, but print journalism still has a place. Exhibit A: *National Geographic*, a magazine with a long history of documenting changes to our planet and highlighting problems, offers up monthly solutions about how we can have things we want while inflicting less harm on the only home we have.

It's not too early to think about what you love, what interests you, and how you can use that passion to make the world a better, cleaner place for you—and everyone who comes next.

AN INEVITABLE
CLEAN-ENERGY REVOLUTION

> Nothing can dim the light
> which shines from within.
>
> —MAYA ANGELOU

Imagine this: it's the year 2050, and big challenges (and opportunities) remain. We still have occasional supersized storms. Sea levels continue to rise, challenging many coastal areas. New seawalls provide protection, but those only go so far. Many people who live near the ocean have had to learn to live with the water instead of trying to hold it back. Some cities, like Miami, Norfolk, and New Orleans, have built water into their city plans, complete with water taxis, floating homes, and flood-proof construction.

That said, some Americans have chosen to move farther inland to escape constant coastal flooding. Others have decided to move away from regions threatened by frequent western fires and searing summer heat. Some parts of the nation have turned out to be more climate-friendly than others. That is our new reality.

But a lot of our hard work is paying off.

We still drive cars, but they're mostly electric, with big, powerful batteries able to go 500 miles on a charge. Gas stations? A few gasoline pumps are available, but service stations now have rows of electrical chargers. Pull up, plug in, and within a few minutes you have 500 miles of range to go anywhere you want to go. A few gasoline-powered cars are still around, driven mainly by older people on weekends, but most of them are in museums now.

Trains, buses, and trucks are mainly electric now too, able to recharge batteries continuously, thanks to new innovative highway surfaces that collect solar power and electrify the vehicles above.

Most airplanes are powered by massive batteries now as well, especially for shorter flights. Bigger, long-haul jets fly across the oceans, powered by biofuels created from corn and other crops. This new generation of jets emits no greenhouse gases into the atmosphere.

The United States no longer uses coal or natural gas to keep the lights on. Millions of us take advantage of wind and solar power, while offering the extra energy we do not need back to other people. Yes, we're able to sell the excess energy we harvest onto a reinvented electric grid! A new generation of smaller, cheaper nuclear plants provides baseline power for the days the sun doesn't shine or the wind doesn't blow, but new technology provides safer power without harmful radioactive waste.

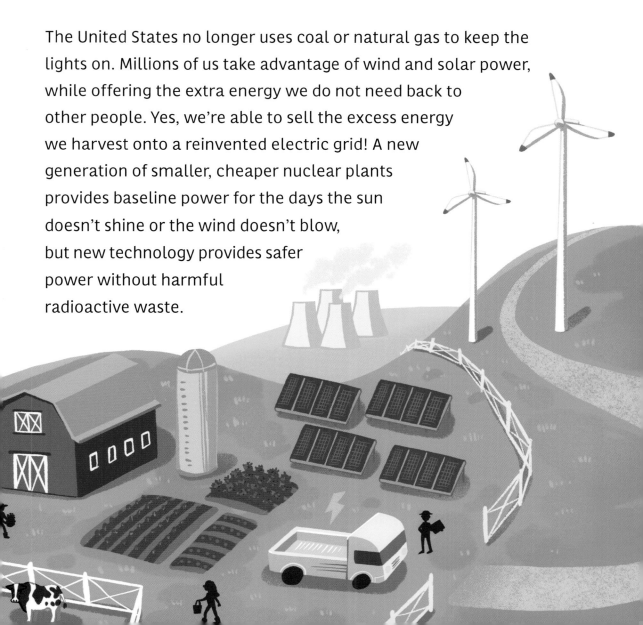

Our homes look roughly the same as they did in the 2020s, but they are much smarter, automatically adjusting to changes in temperature, humidity, and sunlight. Solar collectors built into the roof structure allow homes to produce their own power. More insulation and much stronger materials are able to better withstand floodwaters, hurricane winds, wildfire smoke, intense summer heat, and anything else Mother Nature throws at us.

In 2021, an estimated 24% of all the extra planet-warming CO_2 released into the atmosphere came from agriculture, forestry, and land use. Now, farmers rotate their crops more often to build resilience, and will embrace sustainable standards by planting cover crops, like rye, wheat, barley, and oats, which trap carbon in the ground and reduce the risk of topsoil being washed into the nearest creek by flooding rains. Some farmers have been doing this for hundreds of years to protect their fields and grow healthier crops—a trend that will catch on everywhere. In coming decades, harvests will be even greater than they are today, with more farmers turning to indoor farming and a new generation of fertilizers and pesticides that do not require oil.

In 2050, food looks and tastes the same, but it is easier and cheaper for Americans to buy from local sources, minimizing the need to truck in vegetables and fruit from thousands of miles away.

Americans now recycle like Europeans, separating out not only plastic and paper, but metal and organic waste. In fact, we shun plastic; we make new packaging and bottles from new, recyclable materials that are as strong as plastic but able to break down rapidly over time. Less trash goes into our landfills, which now only accept biodegradable items that do not pollute our land or streams.

The United States races with nations around the world to see who is first to achieve net-zero emissions, a balance between the human-made greenhouse gases being produced and those being removed from the atmosphere. Believe it or not, most countries are close to that remarkable achievement. New technology makes that possible, including devices that suck up excess CO^2 and convert it into sustainable building materials similar to concrete and plastic. We combat deforestation, not only by planting more trees but by erecting huge mechanical trees that suck up CO_2 and emit oxygen. Hundreds of thousands of new businesses compete to create the products and services we want and need, but with less carbon and waste in their daily operations.

Remember, the situation isn't hopeless, and we aren't helpless. The US has tackled huge challenges in the past. By taking advantage of new technology and a growing realization that we can't wait for others to fix our problems, we will reduce pollution, power our cities and towns with cleaner energy sources, and create a new road map for a healthier, happier, more sustainable lifestyle.

A new, clean-energy future is not a sure thing; it is up to you to be part of the solution and make a cleaner world a reality. This is a global challenge. Pollution and global warming don't stop at international borders. We really are all in this together, and it will take a sustained, global approach to turn the tide and find a better, smarter, and cleaner way forward.

Good luck! We are counting on you. Enjoy the journey, and don't be afraid to make your voice heard. When I was growing up, one of my favorite science teachers reminded me that cleaning up the environment and finding smarter, cleaner ways to live aren't a solo act. We are all part of a much bigger chorus—all our voices, skills, and passions blended into one. Now is the time to make your voice heard. Find creative ways to step up and be a part of this incredible journey. Your friends and family will notice and be inspired by your commitment to being part of the solution. Here's a prediction I'm going to get right: this is going to be amazing!

SELECTED BIBLIOGRAPHY

Great Places to Find Out More!

THE BIG PICTURE: CLIMATE CHANGE AND MORE

NASA Global Climate Change (climate.nasa.gov)

NASA Climate Kids (climatekids.nasa.gov)

National Geographic (nationalgeographic.com)

National Oceanic and Atmospheric Administration (noaa.gov)

A RIGHT TO BREATHE CLEAN AIR

World Health Organization (who.int/health-topics/air-pollution)

United States Environmental Protection Agency Acid Rain Students Site (www3.epa.gov/acidrain/education/site_students)

CLEAN WATER IS A HUMAN RIGHT

WWALS Watershed Coalition (wwals.net)

United Nations Water for Life
(un.org/waterforlifedecade/quality.shtml)

US Geological Survey Water Science School
(usgs.gov/special-topic/water-science-school)

SAVE THE OCEANS

Aeon for Ocean
(aeonforocean.org)

Ocean Conservancy
(oceanconservancy.org)

Sea Turtle Conservancy
(conserveturtles.org)

CLEAN ENERGY

National Renewable Energy Laboratory (nrel.gov/about/ehs.html)

US Department of Energy (energy.gov)

MIT Technology Review (technologyreview.com/topic/climate-change)

ACKNOWLEDGMENTS

Over the years I have been invited to talk about weather and climate at hundreds of schools. I always leave these speaking engagements feeling energized, uplifted, and optimistic for the future. Young people have a way of looking at everything, seeing past the negatives to the possibilities. I owe a debt of gratitude to my literary agent, Dawn Frederick, for suggesting that I write a book about the challenges our planet is facing—one geared to younger readers who might want to someday be part of the solutions required to address pollution and climate change. The threats are real, but the opportunities to create a cleaner, more sustainable world are limitless. This book was an attempt to capture some of that optimism and to highlight the amazing kids already doing great things to address environmental challenges today. They are not waiting around; they are stepping up now. We need more of that. Faster.

I am grateful for an encouraging editor that fate put in my path. Elizabeth Schleisman at Beaming Books helped me fine-tune a narrative that would not only lay out the facts but use illustrations to tell these stories, helping young readers absorb the implications while hopefully leaving them upbeat, optimistic, and ready to roll up their sleeves to work together on solutions. That is no small task! Liz was passionate and patient while editing *A Kid's Guide to Saving the Planet*. I am so grateful to have worked with her and her amazing team on this book.

A big thank-you to friend and colleague Dr. John Abraham, a gifted climate scientist at the University of St. Thomas here in the Twin Cities. Not only is John a dedicated father, accomplished professor, and gifted communicator, but he is one of the kindest people I've ever met. Supersmart with a big heart. We need more of that. Dr. Abraham was generous with his time reviewing my manuscript and making sure I got my facts and the science right. I am grateful.

Finally, a thank-you to my first grandchild, Jordan, whose birth in early 2020 was a reminder to me that I have a duty and an obligation to speak up for future generations. One thing is certain in life: we love our kids and our grandkids. We would do anything and everything in our power to make sure they enjoy the same things we did growing up. Jordan is curious, high-energy, and optimistic by nature, with a very well-developed sense of humor. He will need that sense of enthusiasm and an unrelenting can-do spirit in the years to come. We all will, as our children, and their children, work together to clean up Earth, limit future damage, and make sure everyone who comes next has an appreciation for the fragility of our home planet.

Here's a hopeful prediction: my grandson Jordan, the readers, and everyone in their extended families, will grow up acknowledging reality, with a willingness to clean up our messes and face the future with a mixture of resolve, gratitude, and confidence that only we can make things better.

PAUL DOUGLAS is a nationally recognized meteorologist, entrepreneur, and author based in the Twin Cities of Minnesota. He has witnessed the symptoms of a rapidly changing climate show up in extreme weather and has made regular appearances on MSNBC and in The Washington Post. Douglas is the author of *Restless Skies: The Ultimate Weather Book* and coauthor of *Caring for Creation: The Evangelical's Guide to Climate Change and a Healthy Environment*.

CHELEN ÉCIJA is an illustrator and letterer based in sunny Spain. She loves to travel, eat sunflower seeds, and buy new books. She studied Fine Arts in Madrid and Chicago, where she attended The School of the Art Institute and she was an art director in a boutique toy company for a while while living in the USA. Now she is back in Europe, working as a freelance illustrator where she has specialized in her true passion: hand lettering and childrens illustration.